WHAT·DO·WE·KNOW ABOUT SIKHISM·?

BERYL DHANJAL

HODDER
Wayland

an imprint of Hodder Children's Books

First published in 1996 by
Macdonald Young Books

First published in paperback in 2000 by
Hodder Wayland, an imprint of
Hodder Children's Books

© Hodder Wayland 2000

Designer and illustrator: Celia Hart
Commissioning editor: Debbie Fox
Editor: Caroline Arthur
Picture research: Jane Taylor
Consultant: Dr. Eleanor Nesbitt, Warwick Religions and Education Unit,
          University of Warwick.

500 562114

Photograph acknowledgements: Front and back cover: Bipinchandra J Mistry;
Andes Press Agency, p31(b) (Carlos Reyes Manzo); The British Library,
p21(t); Beryl Dhanjal, p16(b); Format Photographers, pp8(l), 24 (Judy
Harrison); Hulton Deutsch, p19(b); The Hutchison Library, p27(t); Magnum
Photos, pp39(b), 41(t) (Raghu Rai), 41(b) (P Marlow); Bipinchandra J Mistry,
endpapers, pp9, 14, 21(b), 23(b), 25(t), 29, 36, 37(t), 37(b); Network
Photographers, pp31(t) (Barry Lewis), 33 (Martin Meyer); Christine Osborne
Pictures, pp8(r), 26, 32, 34, 43; Ann & Bury Peerless, pp13(t), 19(t); Rex
Features, p33; Trip, pp12, 13(b), 15(t), 15(b), 16(t), 17, 18, 20, 22, 23(t), 25(b),
27(b), 28, 29, 30, 35(t), 35(b), 38, 39(t) (Suresh Gavali), 40, 42 (Hélène Rogers).

Printed in Hong Kong by Wing King Tong

A CIP catalogue record for this book
Is available from the British Library.

ISBN: 0 7502 3266 8

Hodder Children's Books
A division of Hodder Headline Ltd
338 Euston Road, London NW1 3BH

Endpapers: A scene from a wall painting of
Guru Nanak's life.

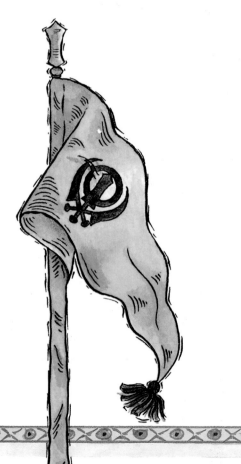

· CONTENTS ·

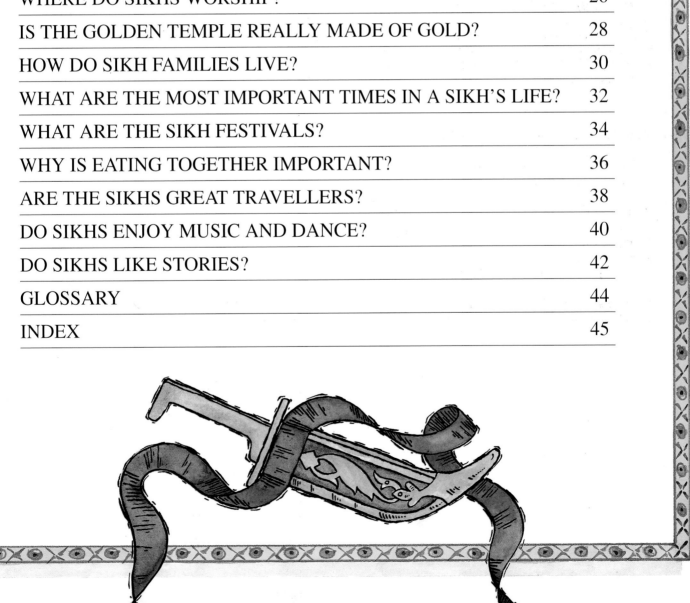

WHO·ARE·THE·SIKHS?

Sikhs believe in one God. They also believe in the ten Gurus (founding teachers) and the Guru Granth Sahib (the holy book prepared by one of the Gurus). Some Sikhs believe that they should also belong to the Khalsa, the special community set up by the tenth Guru (see page 16). But there are many families who have never followed this tradition, while others no longer observe the Khalsa tradition, but still see themselves as Sikhs. The congregation, *sangat*, is very important to Sikhs. They believe that people should meet together. The place where Sikhs meet for religious, social and educational activities is called a *gurdwara*. For example, elderly people may meet, talk and enjoy lunch together at a gurdwara.

THE GURDWARA

The people in this photograph are standing outside their gurdwara. The gurdwara is the Guru's court, just like the court of a king, where the holy book sits on its throne. There are no priests at a gurdwara, though there are Granthis, who look after the holy book and the building. But they are not leaders or teachers. Gurdwaras are usually run by elected committees. Women can be elected to these committees, as they are equal to men. They also have their own group, which usually meets on a weekday afternoon. The women organise activities and eat together.

CHILDREN AT SUNDAY SCHOOL

These British children are at their gurdwara to learn the language spoken by Sikhs in India, Panjabi, and for lessons about the Gurus. No particular day of the week is special for Sikhs. They usually hold meetings, go to gurdwara, have processions and celebrate festivals on whatever day of the week is a public holiday in the country where they live.

Number of gurdwaras in a country

- over 100
- 50 to 100
- 10 to 50
- 1 to 10

SIKHS AROUND THE WORLD

There are about 14 million Sikhs in India (about two per cent of the population, so they are a very small minority). Most Sikh families are originally from India, but a few Sikhs have converted from other religions. Some families have moved to other countries all over the world, especially Britain, the USA and Canada, as you can see on the map. In fact, there are probably a few in most countries.

GURU NANAK'S LEARNERS

In Panjabi, the word *Sikh* means a 'student' or 'learner'. When Guru Nanak, the first Guru, was old, many people came to live near him to hear his teaching. People called them 'Sikhs' – Guru Nanak's learners – which is how the name began.

THE GURU GRANTH SAHIB

The photograph above shows the Sikh holy book, which is called the Guru Granth Sahib. Sikhs see it as their religious teacher and leader and treat it with great respect. In the morning, when it is opened, they look to see what verse is in the top left-hand corner of the page: this verse gives the 'orders for the day'. Sometimes, people ask the Guru Granth Sahib to solve difficult questions. They open the book and read what they find there. They believe that what they read will give them the answer to their problem.

TIMELINE

EVENTS IN SIKHISM

1469	1526	1539	1552–1574	1574–1581	1577
Guru Nanak is born near Lahore. At the age of about 30 he begins teaching. This is the start of Sikhism.	Babur invades India and establishes the Mogul Empire. The Mogul Emperors rule until the 19th century.	Guru Nanak dies. He has already appointed Guru Angad to take over. Guru Angad is said to have developed the Gurmurkhi alphabet.	Guru Amar Das is Guru. He insists that visitors eat a meal together in the Guru's kitchen. From now on, all the Gurus belong to one family.	Guru Ram Das is Guru. He founds the city of Amritsar and has the pool there dug.	The city of Amritsar is founded and becomes an important trading centre.

Guru Nanak

1845–6 1848–9	1839	1799	1780	1700s	1707
Two wars are fought between the Sikhs and the British, who are trying to take over Panjab.	Ranjit Singh dies. For ten years, various groups squabble and try to rule.	Ranjit Singh takes over Lahore, the capital of Panjab, and becomes Emperor. He is a clever ruler who employs people of all religions and nationalities.	Maharaja Ranjit Singh is born. The old leaders are dying out and he takes over their powers.	Panjab is invaded many times from Afghanistan. Various Sikh leaders in Panjab rule different areas. They often fight each other.	Aurangzeb, the last great Mogul Emperor, dies. He, his father and grandfather have been less tolerant and liberal than earlier Mogul princes.
1849–1947 The British rule Panjab. They build roads, railways, schools and hospitals, control flooding rivers and bring in irrigation and electricity.				**Ranjit Singh**	

1873	1890s	1919	1920	1921–1925	1925
The Singh Sabha begins. This is a movement for reforming Sikhism. The leaders say everyone should belong to the Khalsa.	Many Sikhs move to East Africa to work.	People who have come to the festival of Vaisakhi in Amritsar are massacred by the British General Dyer's soldiers in a park called Jallianwala Bagh.	A special committee, the Shiromani Gurdwara Prabandhak Committee, is set up to take charge of gurdwaras.	There are quarrels about who owns and controls gurdwaras. The families who control them claim to own them, but the reformers say they are public property.	The Sikh Gurdwaras Act in India legally defines a Sikh and makes a difference between Sikhs and Hindus. It also says which holy sites belong to Hindus, Muslims and Sikhs.

THE DIVISION OF PANJAB

In 1947, when India became independent from British rule, the Hindus and Muslims each wanted their own country. The border had to run through Panjab, where there were many Hindus and Muslims, but nearly 15 per cent of the people were Sikhs. The new border cut between Lahore and Amritsar. Millions of people had to move: Muslims moved to Pakistan and Hindus and Sikhs to India. They all lost their homes, and many people on both sides were massacred. It is thought that 250,000 people died. After the partition, India and Pakistan were not on friendly terms with each other. It became impossible for Sikhs living in the Indian part of Panjab to visit the sites where the Gurus were born and died, because they were in Pakistan.

Khanda

THE SIKH SYMBOL

A *khanda* is a double-edged sword. It appears in the centre of the symbol which many Sikhs wear and which appears on the Nishan Sahib, the flag of Sikh gurdwaras. The *khanda* has to be sharp on both edges, which symbolises the need to be a soldier and a saint. The curved swords, called *kirpans*, are symbols of spiritual power and authority over people. The circle is a *chakkar*, an ancient Indian weapon, which stands for the one God and the unity of people.

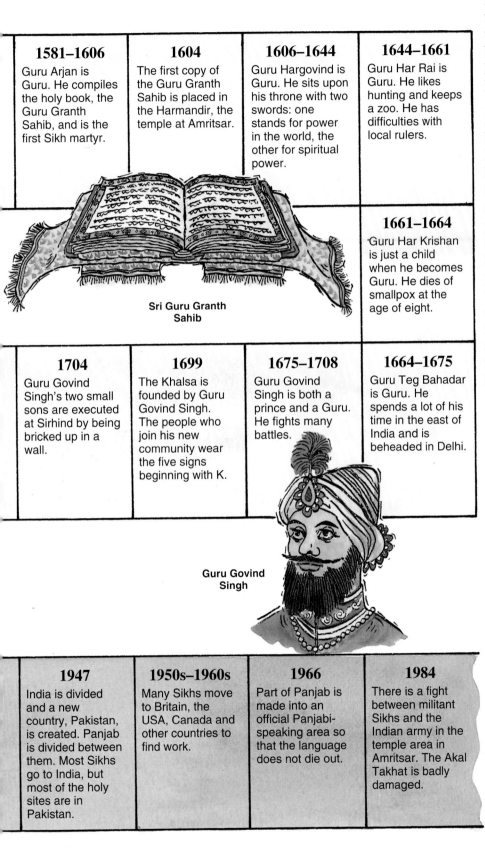

1581–1606	1604	1606–1644	1644–1661
Guru Arjan is Guru. He compiles the holy book, the Guru Granth Sahib, and is the first Sikh martyr.	The first copy of the Guru Granth Sahib is placed in the Harmandir, the temple at Amritsar.	Guru Hargovind is Guru. He sits upon his throne with two swords: one stands for power in the world, the other for spiritual power.	Guru Har Rai is Guru. He likes hunting and keeps a zoo. He has difficulties with local rulers.

Sri Guru Granth Sahib

			1661–1664
			Guru Har Krishan is just a child when he becomes Guru. He dies of smallpox at the age of eight.

1704	1699	1675–1708	1664–1675
Guru Govind Singh's two small sons are executed at Sirhind by being bricked up in a wall.	The Khalsa is founded by Guru Govind Singh. The people who join his new community wear the five signs beginning with K.	Guru Govind Singh is both a prince and a Guru. He fights many battles.	Guru Teg Bahadar is Guru. He spends a lot of his time in the east of India and is beheaded in Delhi.

Guru Govind Singh

1947	1950s–1960s	1966	1984
India is divided and a new country, Pakistan, is created. Panjab is divided between them. Most Sikhs go to India, but most of the holy sites are in Pakistan.	Many Sikhs move to Britain, the USA, Canada and other countries to find work.	Part of Panjab is made into an official Panjabi-speaking area so that the language does not die out.	There is a fight between militant Sikhs and the Indian army in the temple area in Amritsar. The Akal Takhat is badly damaged.

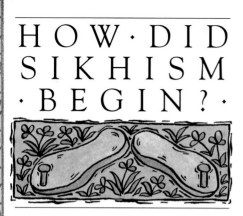

Sikhism began in the area called Panjab, in the north west of India. Guru Nanak, the founder of Sikhism, was born at Nankana Sahib, near Lahore in Panjab, in 1469. Traditional stories tell that at the time of his birth there were signs that someone special had come to Earth. Many people in India believe that everyone has more then one life and is reborn time and again. Sometimes, they believe, special teachers choose to be reborn to help the people of the world. Sikhs say that Guru Nanak was one of these teachers. Guru Nanak showed people a new way to God. He taught about God through poetry, and many people came to hear him teach. These followers became the first Sikhs.

GURU NANAK

The picture on the left is a portrait of Guru Nanak. When Nanak was a young man, he was dreamy and devoted to God. One day, he disappeared into a river. He found himself in God's court, where he was told to teach God's path. The Guru often travelled abroad with his friend Mardana, a Muslim musician. The Guru was a great poet and would sing his poems while Mardana played. When the Guru became old, he settled down and was surrounded by his followers, who set up a small community. He was respected by both Hindus and Muslims. He taught that putting on a show is pointless, and that what happens inside the heart is more important. Ordinary people could avoid being reborn over and over again by looking towards God and trying to become part of Him. This was something that happened not after death but during life.

PANJAB

The name Panjab means 'five rivers'. It is an area where different cultures meet: to the south is Hindu India and to the north are the lands of tribal people, many of whom are Muslims. Most of the places that are important to Sikhs are in Panjab, including the city of Amritsar, the home of the Harmandir Sahib, or Golden Temple (see page 28).

THE MOGUL EMPIRE

In 1526, during Guru Nanak's life, a king called Babur invaded India from the north. He was descended from Tamerlane and Genghis Khan, two very famous warriors. Babur's descendants, called the Moguls, ruled India for many years, during the time of the Sikh Gurus. The five great emperors, Akbar, Humayun, Jahangir, Shah Jahan and Aurangzeb, ruled until 1707. The tenth Guru, Govind Singh, died in 1708. The picture on the right shows Babur and the other descendants of Tamerlane.

GURU NANAK AS A CHILD

Guru Nanak is usually pictured as an old man, so it is nice to see that he was a child! This picture tells a story from his childhood. Nanak was sent to look after his family's cattle. He was thinking about God and let the cows graze in a neighbour's field. The neighbour complained, but when everyone went to look not so much as a blade of grass was nibbled!

MOGUL PRINCES

Babur's descendants were an amazing family. Although they were Muslims, Babur's grandson, Akbar, had Hindu wives. The Moguls loved arts, crafts and architecture, and Akbar's grandson built the famous Taj Mahal. But sometimes they were cruel, especially in punishing their enemies.

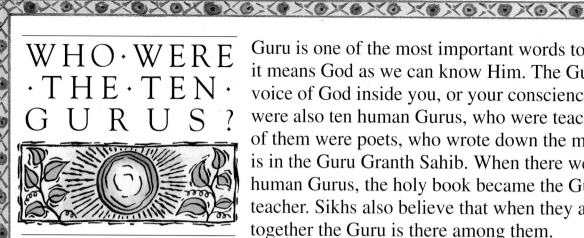

Guru is one of the most important words to a Sikh. First, it means God as we can know Him. The Guru is also the voice of God inside you, or your conscience. But there were also ten human Gurus, who were teachers. Seven of them were poets, who wrote down the message which is in the Guru Granth Sahib. When there were no more human Gurus, the holy book became the Guru, the teacher. Sikhs also believe that when they are gathered together the Guru is there among them.

THE TEN GURUS

This poster shows all ten Gurus. The Gurus were the leaders of the Sikh community. They built towns, and temples such as Harmandir Sahib. They provided hospitals for the people. They started the Guru's kitchen, so that everyone who came to see them could eat together. The fifth Guru, Guru Arjan, and the ninth Guru, Guru Teg Bahadar, were killed while defending their beliefs and are remembered with special affection. The eighth Guru was a child, who died of smallpox when he was eight years old. Schools are often named after him.

PASSING ON THE GURUSHIP

The first three Gurus were not related to each other. The third Guru chose his son-in-law, the husband of his daughter, Bibi Bhaini. She wanted the Guruship to remain in the family, and from then on it did. The Guruship passed from father to son until the eighth Guru, Har Krishan, died in childhood. The ninth Guru was the child's great-uncle, Teg Bahadar, and the tenth was Teg Bahadar's son, Guru Govind Singh. Then the Guruship passed to the holy book.

ੴ ਅ ੲ ਸ ਹ
ਕ ਖ ਗ ਘ ਙ
ਚ ਛ ਜ ਝ ਞ
ਟ ਠ ਡ ਢ ਣ
ਤ ਥ ਦ ਧ ਨ
ਪ ਫ ਬ ਭ ਮ
ਯ ਰ ਲ ਵ ੜ

ALPHABET

The writing used in the Guru Granth Sahib is called Gurmukhi, which means 'from the Guru's mouth'. The alphabet is called Painti, meaning 35, because it has 35 letters. It is written from left to right, and the letters hang down from the line. Many people say that the alphabet was improved by the second Guru.

MIRI AND PIRI

The sixth Guru sat upon a throne with two swords. These, he said, showed spiritual power (*Piri*) and power in the world (*Miri*). In the city of Amritsar, in Panjab, two buildings, the Harmandir and the Akal Takhat, stand for the two kinds of power. In between them are two flagpoles, called Miri and Piri, as you can see on the right.

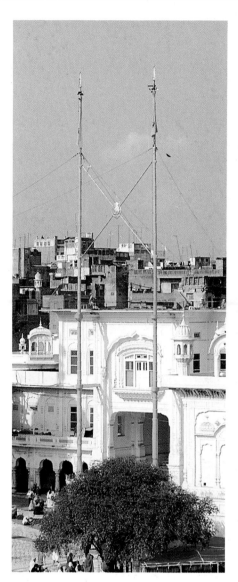

OFFERING WATER

Here, water is offered to passers-by at the gurdwara that marks the spot where the eighth Guru died, in Delhi. India is a hot place, and it is kind to offer cool water to all. Guru Govind Singh once saw a man who gave water to everyone on a battlefield. When the Guru asked him if he had helped the enemy, the water carrier said that he had not seen enemies, he had seen the Guru in everyone.

The Khalsa is a community of Sikhs set up by the tenth Guru, Govind Singh. The word *khalsa* means land, which was under the direct control of a ruler: the Khalsa were people who had a direct relationship with the Guru. There are no priests. The Guru said that the Khalsa were his own body. He expected members of the Khalsa to love God night and day and to think of nothing else. Members of the Khalsa have to wear special signs and follow rules of behaviour.

GURU GOVIND SINGH
Guru Govind Singh was a hero who lived like a prince, with a royal court, elephants and soldiers. He enjoyed hunting and fighting. He taught that it was right to use military force to defend justice. One way he described God was as a sword, calling Him 'Great Steel' and 'Great Death'

Double-edged sword

FOUNDING THE KHALSA
The photograph below is of a relief from the Golden Temple, showing the story of how the Khalsa was founded. Guru Govind Singh asked for five volunteers. He took each man into a tent. He also took a sword. There was a dreadful swish and a thudding sound, and blood flowed out from under the tent. But then he brought out the five men and they were whole. He called them the *Panj Piare*, the Five Beloved Ones. Guru Govind then told them to initiate him, so that he was a member too. One of his wives was passing with some sugar candy, and this was added to water and stirred with a double-edged sword. The mixture is known as *amrit* and is still used to initiate members of the Khalsa.

THE FIVE 'K's

Sikhs believe that when the Khalsa was formed, Guru Govind Singh gave rules of behaviour to the people. He also told them to wear five signs to show they were members. You can still see Sikhs wearing them today. They are:

kes – uncut hair. This means all body hair

kirpan – a sword with a curved blade

kangha – a comb

kara – a steel bangle worn on the wrist of the right hand

kachh – an under-garment.

SINGHS AND KAURS

When men joined the Khalsa they were given the title 'Singh', which means 'Lion'. Many warriors in India used this title. Women were called 'Kaur', meaning 'Princess'. Nowadays, children in Sikh families are often given these names anyway, even if they are not members of the Khalsa. Unlike English names, Sikh names can be for either boys or girls. So Amarjit Singh is a boy and Amarjit Kaur is a girl. Some families use Singh and Kaur as surnames.

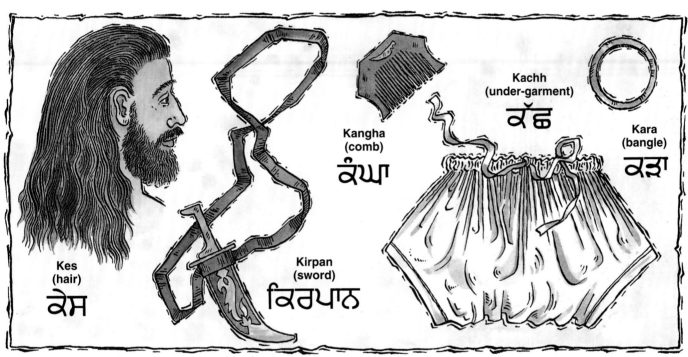

Kes
(hair)
ਕੇਸ

Kirpan
(sword)
ਕਿਰਪਾਨ

Kangha
(comb)
ਕੰਘਾ

Kachh
(under-garment)
ਕੱਛ

Kara
(bangle)
ਕੜਾ

TURBANS

You probably know that Sikh men wear turbans, but it is not one of the special signs the Sikhs were told to wear. This turban shop sells turban cloths in lots of different colours. White can stand for old age and mourning, so people never give a white turban as a gift. Some blue or orange turbans are worn to show the person's political beliefs. There are different ways of wearing turbans. Some people fold them neatly and some have enormous boat shapes. Guru Govind Singh wore beautiful jewels on his.

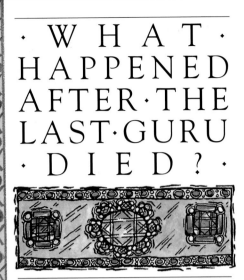

· W H A T · HAPPENED AFTER · THE LAST · GURU · DIED ? ·

Guru Govind Singh, the tenth Guru, died in 1708, just a year after the last of the great Mogul Emperors, Aurangzeb. After Aurangzeb's death, there was no-one to be a strong ruler. During the 18th century, there was no peace in Panjab. There were invasions and battles. Sikh leaders fought the invaders from Afghanistan and Iran, but they often fought each other, too. The invaders attacked the city of Amritsar. Three times they pulled down the Harmandir, and sometimes they demolished the whole city. They even ploughed it up. But the Sikhs hid, then came out, drove the invaders away and rebuilt everything even more beautifully than before.

BABA DIP SINGH

One famous Sikh hero is a scholar called Baba Dip Singh. When he heard that the invaders were coming, he took his sword and went to fight. Some people say that his head was chopped off – but, even so, he fought his way to Amritsar, holding his head in one hand and his sword in the other. This photograph shows the spot beside the temple where he died. People still put flowers there.

MAHARAJA RANJIT SINGH

The picture on the left shows the court of Maharaja Ranjit Singh, a great Sikh ruler. He captured Lahore, the capital of Panjab, in 1799, when he was only 18. He was ugly, marked by scars from smallpox. But he was also witty, clever and full of life and curiosity. He loved horses, war, women and power. The Maharaja gave huge amounts of money and gold to the Harmandir. He also gave money to a Muslim who had spent a lifetime creating a beautiful Quran, and gold to decorate a Hindu temple in Varanasi. He said that God had given him only one eye so that he should look at all religions equally.

Zamzama

RANJIT SINGH'S COURT

Ranjit Singh employed more than 50 Europeans and Americans. The Governor of Peshawar was an American, who whistled 'Yankee Doodle Dandy' as he dressed, but he used to hang people from the minaret of the local mosque. Other Westerners were employed to train the army, but the Panjabis didn't like drill and said it was a 'fool's ballet'.

ZAMZAMA

Zamzama is a very large cannon, which belonged to Maharaja Ranjit Singh. Nowadays, it stands in Lahore, in the middle of the Grand Trunk Road, the main route across India. Indians believe that whoever has Zamzama rules Panjab. If you read *Kim*, by the British writer Rudyard Kipling, you will find Zamzama there.

THE BRITISH RAJ

In the early 1800s, the British ruled a lot of India. One day, Ranjit Singh saw a map. 'What does the red colour stand for?' he asked. 'Red marks the British land,' he was told. 'One day it will all be red!' he said. When Ranjit Singh died, there were wars between the Sikhs and the British. In 1849, the British took over Panjab and ruled it until 1947. This period is called 'the Raj'. The photograph on the left shows Sikh soldiers in the Indian army during the Raj.

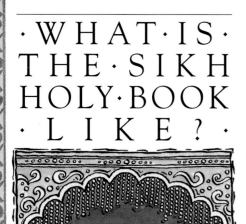

· WHAT · IS · THE · SIKH HOLY · BOOK · LIKE ? ·

The Sikh holy book is called Sri Guru Granth Sahib. *Sri* and *Sahib* are words used to show respect, like calling the book 'Sir'. The book was put together by Guru Arjan, the fifth Guru. It contains poems by the first five Sikh Gurus, the ninth Guru and 35 other holy men from northern India. Some of these came from Hindu backgrounds, and a few were Muslim, but they all taught the same message, that people should love God. The first copy of the book was placed in the Harmandir in Amritsar in 1604.

MERGING FLAMES

When one Guru died and another came, the body was different but the Guru the same. It was like flames merging when two candles are put together. The same spirit is in the book.

Lamps with merging flames

PUTTING THE GRANTH TO BED

Because the book is accepted as the Guru, it is greatly respected and treated as if it were a person. It is placed on a throne and surrounded by symbols of royalty. It is put to bed at night and got up in the morning. This photograph shows a Guru Granth Sahib being put to bed. The book is carefully wrapped up when it is not in use and is transported respectfully on the top of the head.

HANDWRITTEN GURU GRANTH SAHIB

This beautiful Guru Granth Sahib is unique, because it is so decorated. The first page, which you can see here, shows Guru Nanak's basic belief, his poem describing God. It says, 'There is one God. He is the Truth. He is the Creator, and is without fear or hate. He is beyond time, is not born and does not die to be born again. He is known by His grace.'

  ## IDENTICAL PAGES

The Guru Granth Sahib has 1,430 pages. All copies are exactly alike, so the same words always appear on the same page. This makes it easy to refer to particular pieces of writing. There are no stories in the book, just poems praising God.

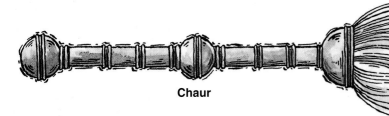

Chaur

THE CHAUR

The *chaur*, or fan, is a symbol of royalty. It is waved over the Guru Granth Sahib to show respect. It is not really a fly whisk, though some people call it that! It is never used to swat flies.

READING THE GURU GRANTH SAHIB

Any member of the congregation or the Granthi may read from the Guru Granth Sahib if they are able and wish to. The book is read aloud so that everyone can hear, and some gurdwaras have sound systems so that the reading can be heard elsewhere in the building. The reading stops and starts during the day, with one person taking over where the last one left off. The reader usually waves the *chaur* and holds a handkerchief to avoid sneezing or coughing over the book.

WHAT·DO ·SIKHS· BELIEVE?

Guru Nanak said that people should look towards God and not stay bound up in their own selves. Sikhs believe that humans must love God and obey Him as a child obeys a father. The more they praise God and devote themselves to Him, the closer they will become to Him. Sikhs do not believe in rewards after death. What they try to do is to become lost in God, rather like salt dissolved in water, in this life. They also believe in living a good life. One important thing that Sikhs say is: 'Meditate on the Name of God, earn an honest living, and share what you have with others.'

SIKHS AT WORK
Sikhs believe that it is important to have a job and work hard. They believe in earning an honest living and sharing it with others. They think it is bad to beg. Sikhs like to do jobs that help people, and many Sikhs are doctors, like the one in the photograph on the right.

THE NAME
Many Sikhs repeat again and again the names of God: *Satnam*, which means 'True Name', and *Wahiguru*, which means 'Wonderful Lord'. They believe this brings them closer to God. You can see these names below, written in Gurmurkhi.

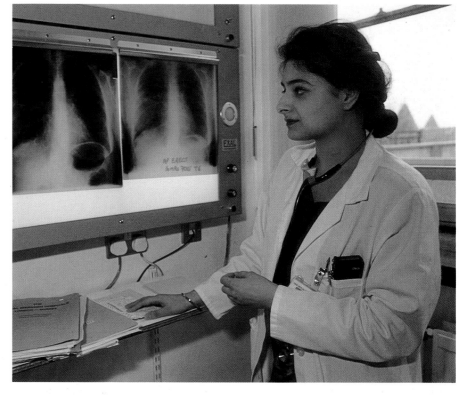

Satnam

ਵਾਹਿਗੁਰੂ

Wahiguru

THERE IS ONE GOD
This symbol means 'There is one God'. It is made up of a number 1 and the symbol *oankar*, which means 'God'. It comes at the very beginning of the Guru Granth Sahib and also begins every poem in the book. It reminds Sikhs of the one God.

Ik Oankar

SACRED LETTERS
There can be no pictures of the Sikh God, but names for him can be written down. Because of this, Sikhs tend to treat any paper with writing on it with great respect, and dispose of it very carefully. Many people cannot read Gurmurkhi writing, but they know it is the Guru's sacred letters and might even include the name of God. In particular, people do not stand on paper or use it to wrap up rubbish.

GIVING FOOD

Service to others and charity are very important in Sikhism. Sikhs believe they should share with others all the good things they are given by God. This means sharing with everyone, not just other Sikhs. These Sikhs in London are offering drinks to passers-by who are taking part in a procession to celebrate Guru Nanak's birthday, and to anyone else who happens to be passing, Sikh or not. Sikhs often offer drinks and snacks to passing processions. Sometimes, they also hand out food and drink to other marchers, even if these are not Sikh or religious.

Mala

DOING SERVICE

Seva, meaning service, is usually service to the community. Sikhs believe that being part of a congregation means more than just giving money. *Seva* can be cleaning, cooking, preparing or serving food in the gurdwara. It might be minding and cleaning other people's shoes when they leave them at the entrance. It is usually hard menial work. These men at a gurdwara in India are cleaning pots and pans with sand after a meal.

THE MALA

Mala means 'garland' or 'necklace'. Some Sikhs use malas like this one for prayer. They are often made of wool, and they have 108 knots or beads. Some people have small ones with 29 knots. Many Sikhs do not approve of malas: they agree with Guru Amar Das, who said that doing good deeds sincerely was the best way to become closer to God.

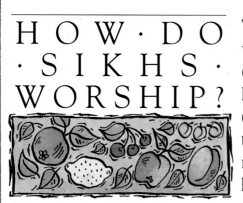

The Guru Granth Sahib is at the centre of all Sikh worship. Once a week, there is a service called Diwan (court), which usually lasts for at least two or three hours. The Guru Granth Sahib is opened and the Ragis (musicians) sing *kirtan* (the hymns). There might be a talk or an explanation of one of the Gurus' poems by a member of the congregation. Speakers may refer to history, stories and sayings. They may respectfully mention other religions, too. At the end of the Diwan, *karah prasad* should be offered to everyone. Everyone then moves to the *langar*, or Guru's kitchen, for the communal meal (see pages 36–37).

PRAYER BOOK
Sikhs have a small prayer book, containing daily prayers. The prayers are from the Guru Granth Sahib, but people need the small book because a Guru Granth Sahib cannot be used for everyday, informal reading. There are prayers to read before dawn, prayers to read at regular times during the day and prayers to read at bedtime. People keep the book wrapped up, and wash their hands before handling it.

Collection box

REMOVING SHOES
Sikhs remove their shoes before they approach a Guru Granth Sahib. Many also wash their feet. A worshipper may run his hand along the threshold to collect dust that has fallen from holy feet and spread it on his forehead.

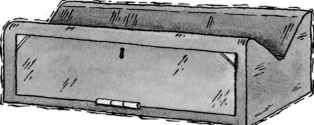

Shoes of worshippers

PRESENTATIONS
In front of the Guru Granth Sahib, there is often a collection box for people to give gifts of money. Other people bring food or milk to present to the Guru. In some gurdwaras, there are crates beside the *manji* (the throne) to hold the milk that is brought in. Food stays in front of the holy book for a while and then goes to the *langar*.

ARDAS

Ardas is the prayer that begins or ends every ritual. It is the only prayer used in gurdwaras that does not come from the Guru Granth Sahib. Ardas is said facing the throne of the Guru Granth Sahib. First, it calls to mind the Gurus and historic events. Then there is a prayer for the Khalsa and for all of humanity. There is also room to ask for help and comfort for people who need it.

READING

Sometimes Sikhs hold an *akhand path*, an unbroken reading of the whole Guru Granth Sahib. This is often done on a special occasion. It takes 48 hours to read the entire book, and it is done by relay teams. If a team start on Friday morning, they finish on Sunday. Anyone who is able and would like to can take part.

BOWING

This Sikh is bowing towards the Guru Granth Sahib to show respect. When they go into the gurdwara, people bow, make their presentation and retreat, without turning their back and without disturbing others. They then sit facing the Guru Granth Sahib, but never point their feet at it.

WHERE · DO · SIKHS · WORSHIP?

Sikhs can worship anywhere. What makes a place special is the holy book. The presence of the Guru Granth Sahib turns a school, hall, or any space into a gurdwara. The name 'gurdwara' means a doorway to the Guru, because it lets people move closer to God. A Guru Granth Sahib can be placed almost anywhere, but a canopy should be put up and a throne provided for the book to rest on. The canopy can be a temporary cloth one: for example, it could be tacked to the picture rail in a house.

Nishan Sahib

GURDWARA

This brand new gurdwara in Australia has been built by the local Sikh congregation. Gurdwaras in India are always specially built, as are more and more gurdwaras in other countries. But when Sikhs move to a new country or town, it is often a while before they are able to build their own gurdwara. Houses, cinemas that have closed down and even disused churches have been used in places where there is no special building.

MOBILE WORSHIP

People say that, back in history, Sikhs worshipped on horseback as they charged along. Sikhs should worship wherever they are: there are no special sacred places and they do not go on pilgrimages. Sikhs believe that everywhere is sacred, for the best way to understand something of God is through seeing His creation.

FLAGPOLE

There are always flagpoles outside gurdwaras. In fact, most Indian religious buildings have flags outside, to tell people what they are and so that people can see them from a long way off. Gurdwara flagpoles are wrapped in orange-coloured cloth and have an orange Nishan Sahib pennant flying from the top. This has a dark blue Khanda emblem on it. At the top is a double-edged sword.

RUMALAS

Rumalas are special cloths which are draped around the Guru Granth Sahib and are used to cover it when it is not actually being read. People bring splendid new rumalas made of rich material and embroidered with gold thread as gifts for the Guru.

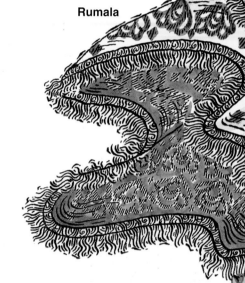

Rumala

WORSHIP AT HOME

Some people keep a Guru Granth Sahib at home. If they do, the book has a special room, where people can treat it with proper respect. Most ordinary people do not have space to keep a Guru Granth Sahib at home all the time, and do not feel able to look after it properly. However, many do have an *akhand path* (an unbroken reading of the whole book) in their home. They may have this done once a year, or when there is a special occasion, either happy (such as a wedding or a baby's birth) or sad (such as a funeral).

INSIDE THE GURDWARA

Inside the gurdwara, the room is organised like the court of an Indian king. The Guru Granth Sahib sits on a throne at the front. The *karah prasad* (see page 36) is kept beside the Guru Granth Sahib and the Ragis (musicians) sit on the other side, facing the *sangat* (the congregation). The members of the congregation sit on the floor, at a lower level than the book. Men sit on one side and women on the other. (There is no religious reason for this: it is a social custom.) Gurdwaras do not have pictures, because it is said that the true picture of the Guru is in the poetry of the holy book.

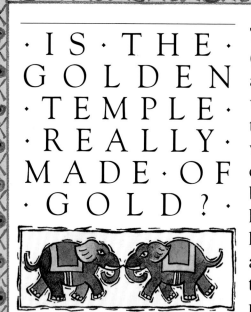

·IS·THE· GOLDEN ·TEMPLE· ·REALLY· MADE·OF ·GOLD?·

The real name of the Golden Temple is Harmandir Sahib (God's temple) or Darbar Sahib (God's court). It is not actually made of gold, but the top part is covered with very pure gold. The first part to be built was the pool, on the orders of Guru Ram Das. There is a story that a woman left her sick husband near the pool. He saw black crows dip into the water and come out white, so he bathed and was made well. Later, Guru Arjan decided to have a temple built in the middle of the pool. The temple has four doors, to show that people from all directions are welcome. Most Indian temples are built high above the ground. At Harmandir Sahib, even the high and mighty have to descend stairs to enter.

THE GOLDEN TEMPLE

The Harmandir was built by Guru Arjan in 1588, but it was demolished three times by invaders during the 18th century. The Sikhs always rebuilt it with great energy. The present temple was built in 1776 and became the Golden Temple when Maharaja Ranjit Singh gave masses of gold to decorate it. There are three copies of the Guru Granth Sahib inside: one downstairs, one upstairs and one under the dome. Although Sikhs do not go on pilgrimages, they do enjoy visiting the temple. It is a beautiful place, with a wonderful atmosphere, and exquisite music is played.

INSCRIPTION

This inscription on the gold above the main door quotes Guru Nanak's description of God. It also says, 'The great Guru in his wisdom looked upon Maharaja Ranjit Singh as his humble servant and caused him to do many acts of service for the temple.' Other inscriptions show that many of the people who gave the gold were Hindus.

GOLD

The Harmandir is covered with gilded copper and also decorated with pure gold. It is estimated that there are about 162 kilograms of gold, most of which was given by Maharaja Ranjit Singh. It is cleaned with ordinary washing powder, and the shine comes from energetic polishing.

DECORATION

Much of the decoration on the walls inside the Harmandir Sahib shows plants and animals, like these. Skilled Hindu, Muslim and Sikh artists worked together to create it. Guru Nanak never grew tired of nature: he said it was a way of knowing God.

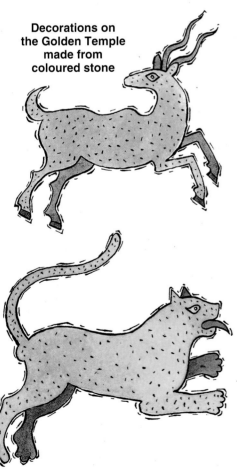

Decorations on the Golden Temple made from coloured stone

BATHING

People are always very keen to bathe at Amritsar, as the Sikhs in this photograph are doing. The reason is that *amrit* means nectar and *sar* means a pool, so the name of the city means 'the pool of nectar'. This nectar is supposed to make bathers live forever.

H O W · D O · S I K H · FAMILIES · L I V E ? ·

Family life is important to Sikhs. They believe that people should marry and care for their families. They should work to feed themselves and to give to others. They should live normal, sensible lives, trying to get closer to God without shutting themselves off from everyday life. For Sikhs, marriage is the most important stage of life. Traditionally, sons stayed with their father in the family home, and they all worked together, lived together, shared the expenses and ate together. When women married, they joined their husbands' families. Eventually, these extended families would become too large and would split up.

EXTENDED FAMILY

In India, 80 per cent of people live in the countryside. There, the extended family is ideal, as everyone can help with growing food. But people in cities, too, find a big family splendid for running a business. Everyone enjoys having their relatives around them. The family in the photograph live in Amritsar, but they have relatives in other towns in India and in Britain. Sikhs do not marry their relatives or people from their family village, so they end up with lots of relations spread over a wide area.

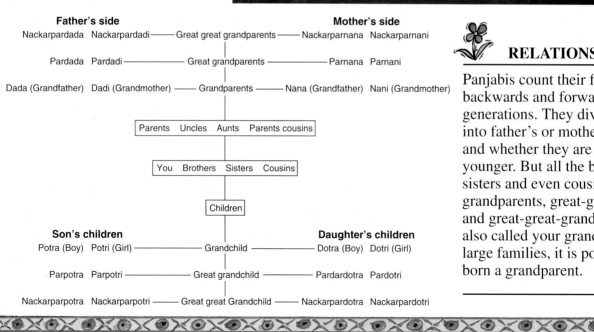

Father's side				Mother's side	
Nackarpardada	Nackarpardadi	Great great grandparents	Nackarparnana	Nackarparnani
Pardada	Pardadi	Great grandparents	Parnana	Parnani
Dada (Grandfather)	Dadi (Grandmother)	Grandparents	Nana (Grandfather)	Nani (Grandmother)

Parents	Uncles	Aunts	Parents cousins

You	Brothers	Sisters	Cousins

Children

Son's children				Daughter's children	
Potra (Boy)	Potri (Girl)	Grandchild	Dotra (Boy)	Dotri (Girl)
Parpotra	Parpotri	Great grandchild	Pardardotra	Pardotri
Nackarparpotra	Nackarparpotri	Great great Grandchild	Nackarpardotra	Nackarpardotri

RELATIONSHIPS

Panjabis count their families backwards and forwards four generations. They divide relatives into father's or mother's sides, and whether they are older or younger. But all the brothers, sisters and even cousins of your grandparents, great-grandparents and great-great-grandparents are also called your grandparents. In large families, it is possible to be born a grandparent.

THE COMMUNITY

Years ago, in India, villagers all worked together, helping each other. Now, times have changed and people live different sorts of lives. But Sikhs still like to meet other people and often arrange parties and outings. Sikhs do not spend all their time being serious, and they are no different from the rest of the world. They enjoy the same pleasures as other people. Is there anyone who wouldn't enjoy a day at Blackpool and ice-cream?

SMALL FAMILY

In Western countries such as Britain, Canada and the United States, it is not usually practical for Sikh families to live together. The houses are not designed for large groups. Sikh families live very much like their neighbours. This family in London are enjoying seeing the sights.

CARROM

Carrom is a traditional Indian game played by two or four players. The aim is to flick counters into the pockets with the striker. The player to pocket all the counters of their chosen colour, and then the Queen, wins. It can get very exciting. Sikhs enjoy many games. They also love sport, especially team games such as hockey and cricket.

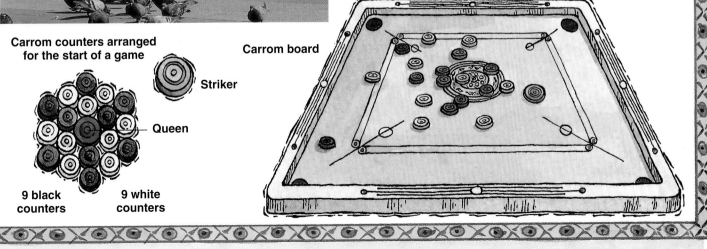

Carrom counters arranged for the start of a game

Striker

Queen

9 black counters

9 white counters

Carrom board

WHAT·ARE THE·MOST IMPORTANT TIMES·IN·A SIKH'S·LIFE?

The most important times in anyone's life are births, deaths and marriages, and this is true for Sikhs, too. Marriage is the most splendid time for any Indian family. Before the wedding, there are many traditional rituals to bring the two families together. Some Sikhs have a Khalsa initiation ceremony, called taking *pahul*. This reminds them of the founding of the Khalsa. Wearing the five Ks, the new members are given *amrit* (nectar) to drink and it is scattered on them. They promise to keep Sikh discipline. When a Sikh dies, the body is cremated: although people naturally feel sad, they do not make a big display of their grief.

HENNA PATTERNS

A bride's patterned hand

Before a wedding, the bride's family make her beautiful. One old tradition is to decorate her hands and feet with patterns painted on with henna, a reddish dye. Some artistic people make up the patterns, but you can buy stencils.

THE WEDDING CEREMONY

In India, weddings are held in the bride's home, but they may be held in any large space. The most important thing is that the Guru Granth Sahib must be there. As you can see in the photo above, the couple's scarves are tied together, and they walk four times clockwise round the Guru Granth Sahib. The bride follows the groom. A special hymn about marriage written by Guru Ram Das is sung. After the fourth circle, they become husband and wife.

WEDDING ADORNMENTS

The bridegroom leaves home wearing a veil made of red material and tinsel. The bride wears special red and white bangles. She also wears a dangly ornament on her wrist. The necklaces, earrings and other jewellery she wears are made of pure gold.

Bridegroom's veil

Bride's ornament

HAPPY COLOURS

Indian brides would not think of wearing white dresses. White stands for old age and mourning. Red is the colour for happy ceremonies, so brides wear a red sari, or *salwar kamiz*, the trouser suit worn by Panjabi women. Pink or apricot are popular, as these are also lucky. Men often wear smart suits, though sometimes they wear an Indian jacket with a high collar and loose trousers.

Bride's bangles

DEGREE CEREMONY

Sikh means a learner, and Sikhs believe education is vital. Sikh children are generally encouraged to reach the highest level possible, like this girl getting her university degree.

A NEW BABY

Here, you can see a Sikh family with a new baby. Some people read a prayer by Guru Nanak into a new baby's ear and go to the gurdwara for a blessing. Many choose a name by having the Guru Granth Sahib opened and taking a name beginning with the first letter on the page. They give the baby a taste of *amrit* and sprinkle some on it. They celebrate and give sweets to friends. Many celebrate the birth of a son more than a daughter, though Sikhs should welcome and care for girls, too.

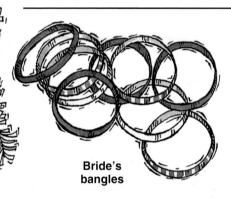

·WHAT·ARE· ·THE·SIKH· FESTIVALS?

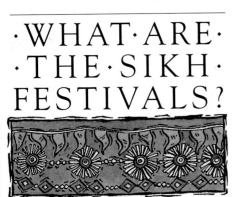

The Sikhs have two kinds of festivals. There are *melas* – fairs – and *Gurpurbs,* the anniversaries of Gurus' births and deaths. As there were ten Gurus, there are a lot of Gurpurbs. The most popular is Guru Nanak's birthday, which most Sikhs celebrate, and some remember Guru Govind Singh's birthday, too. The deaths of Guru Teg Bahadar and Guru Arjan, who died defending their faith, are also remembered. The melas, such as Vaisakhi, are traditional fairs, when people enjoy themselves.

VAISAKHI

Vaisakhi is the anniversary of the founding of the Khalsa, and is when new members are initiated. It usually falls on 13 April. The other ceremony carried out at Vaisakhi is washing the gurdwara flagpole. The pole is taken down and the old wrappings are taken off. The flagpole is washed in yoghurt, which is believed to purify it. Then the pole is re-wrapped, a new Nishan Sahib is put on top, and the pole is raised back into place, as you can see in the photograph above.

Nishan Sahib

DIWALI

Diwali is the Indian festival of light, when children light lamps and candles. They are given presents and sweets. They also enjoy letting off fireworks. In Amritsar, the Golden Temple is lit up and the special treasury is opened for all the treasures to be displayed.

THE GURU'S TASSELS

The story Sikhs tell for Diwali is not the same as the Hindu one. Sikhs remember the time when the sixth Guru was in prison. The Emperor said that he should be released, but the Guru asked about the other prisoners. Could they be freed, too? The Emperor said that as many as could pass through a narrow passage holding the Guru's clothing could go. So the Guru ordered a long cloak with very, very long tassels on the end of it: holding these, 52 men walked through the passage and were freed!

GURU NANAK'S BIRTHDAY

Guru Nanak's birthday, in November, and other Gurpurbs are usually celebrated by taking the Guru Granth Sahib out in procession. It is placed on a specially decorated float or lorry and taken round the town. Five people dressed as the Five Beloved Ones head the procession, while other people carry flags and banners. Balloons and streamers may be hung up beside the road. Children and old people sometimes travel on other lorries. Along the route of the procession, other Sikhs may hand out food and drinks to passing members of the public.

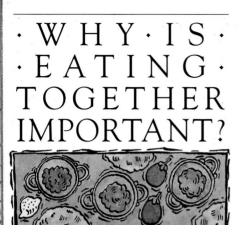

The Guru's kitchen at a gurdwara is called the *langar*, which means 'the anchor'. The same word is used for the food served there. It was started by Guru Nanak to show that Sikhs do not believe in a caste system. The food may be given, cooked and served by anyone, and everyone eats together. The food cooked in gurdwaras is vegetarian. (Sikhs do not have to be vegetarians. The Gurus were famous hunters. If Sikhs are vegetarian, it is their own choice, not a religious rule.) Sometimes, Sikhs organise food for needy people such as refugees.

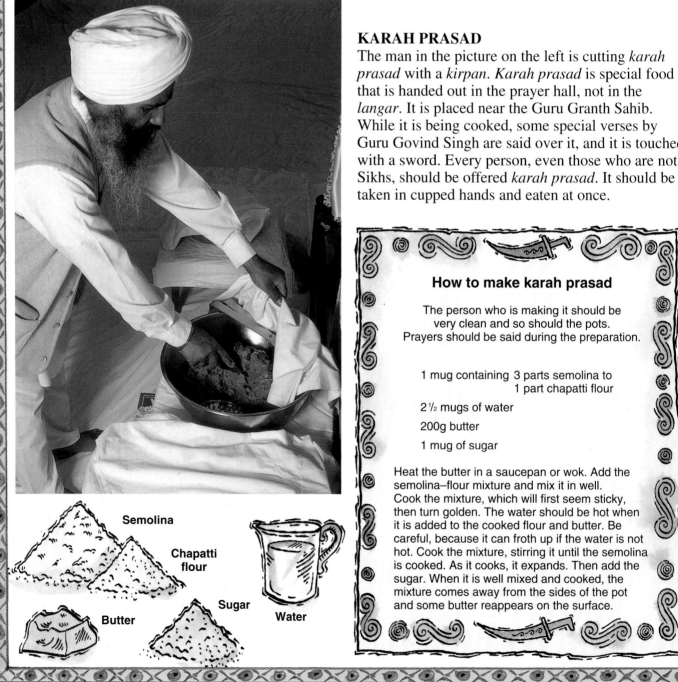

KARAH PRASAD

The man in the picture on the left is cutting *karah prasad* with a *kirpan*. *Karah prasad* is special food that is handed out in the prayer hall, not in the *langar*. It is placed near the Guru Granth Sahib. While it is being cooked, some special verses by Guru Govind Singh are said over it, and it is touched with a sword. Every person, even those who are not Sikhs, should be offered *karah prasad*. It should be taken in cupped hands and eaten at once.

How to make karah prasad

The person who is making it should be very clean and so should the pots. Prayers should be said during the preparation.

1 mug containing 3 parts semolina to 1 part chapatti flour

2½ mugs of water

200g butter

1 mug of sugar

Heat the butter in a saucepan or wok. Add the semolina–flour mixture and mix it in well. Cook the mixture, which will first seem sticky, then turn golden. The water should be hot when it is added to the cooked flour and butter. Be careful, because it can froth up if the water is not hot. Cook the mixture, stirring it until the semolina is cooked. As it cooks, it expands. Then add the sugar. When it is well mixed and cooked, the mixture comes away from the sides of the pot and some butter reappears on the surface.

Semolina

Chapatti flour

Butter

Sugar

Water

PANGAT

Here, people are being given the food cooked in the *langar*. This food is always eaten sitting in lines, which is called *pangat*. In hot countries, the people may sit on the ground and eat off leaves, which take the place of plates. At big gurdwaras, there may be stainless steel trays, like the ones in the photograph. In Western countries, there may be tables and chairs. What matters is that people should sit and eat in lines, so that no-one is sitting at a high table or in a special position and seems more important than anyone else. People of all castes, classes and religions sit in one line and at the same level.

COOKING IN THE GURDWARA

Cooking food is part of *seva*, or service to the community. Any Sikh, of either sex and from any background, should be allowed to offer, prepare and serve food. The pots in the gurdwara are big, so you need strong arms to stir them, as you can see in the photograph on the left. People may donate food to the gurdwara on special occasions or anniversaries. They may also donate money whenever they go to the gurdwara, so that food can be bought.

ARE·THE ·SIKHS· ·GREAT· TRAVELLERS?

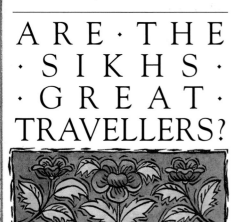

Panjabis have always been great travellers. The ancient trade routes from the West to China and from central Asia to India pass through or close to Panjab. The Sikh Gurus, in particular, were not men who stayed all their lives in one spot. They travelled all over the place. Since then, especially over the last 100 years, many Sikhs have moved away from Panjab. Men have gone to trade and to find jobs in other lands. They have travelled with the army. Many women have travelled because they have married men who live abroad.

GURU NANAK'S TRAVELS

Guru Nanak is said to have travelled all over India and also abroad, to Baghdad and Mecca. There are many tales of his travels. In these, the Guru usually meets wicked people or creatures, like this nasty demon, who was going to cook the Guru's friend, Mardana. But they are won over by his teaching and become Sikhs. In one tale, he visited two villages. In one, the people were hospitable, but in the other they were horrible. When he left, the good people's village was destroyed. When Mardana asked why, the Guru said that the good people should go into the world and spread their goodness, but the bad people should stay where they were!

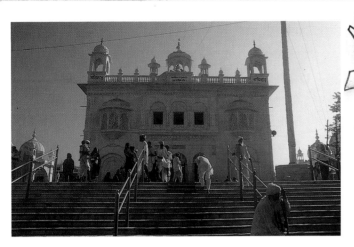

NANDED

It was not only Guru Nanak who travelled. The other Gurus journeyed round Panjab and went as far as Eastern India. Guru Govind Singh died in Western India, at a place called Nanded. Maharaja Ranjit Singh built a gurdwara there, which you can see in the photograph. The Guru's weapons and possessions are kept there.

SIKH EMIGRANTS

In 1914, the Canadian government would not let Sikhs go to live there. A businessman hired a ship, and 376 people (all but 30 were Sikhs) went to Canada to try to change the law. But they were not even allowed to land, and had to return to India.

THE FIVE TAKHATS

There are five Takhats, or Sikh 'thrones', spread all round India. The oldest is the Akal Takhat, which Guru Hargovind built as his court in Amritsar. The others are important places in the life of Guru Govind Singh. Patna is his birthplace, Nanded in Maharashtra is where he died and Keshgarh is where the Khalsa was founded. Damdama Sahib, which means the resting place, is where the final Guru Granth Sahib was dictated. The Takhats have heads called Jathedars, who are paid officials. They are often described as 'high priests', but no one is high in Sikhism and there are no priests.

COMMUNITY PROJECTS

Here, Sikhs are helping with a building project. Sikhs think it is important to help their community. They travel a long way to take part in this kind of project. They may wear their best clothes to travel in and keep them on while they carry soil or do other physical and dirty work, as these people are doing. Often, whole buildings are built or repaired by volunteers. Probably the biggest and most popular project is when the pool at Amritsar is cleaned out.

·DO·SIKHS· ·ENJOY· MUSIC·AND ·DANCE?·

The classical Indian musical system, the *raga*, which creates the mood of the music, is very important to Sikhism. The Guru Granth Sahib is arranged according to the raga that should go with each poem. This shows that the Gurus understood music and thought it mattered. The *Gurbani* (the Gurus' poetry) is sung in gurdwaras as hymns called *kirtan*. The music is supposed to be simple, so that everyone can take part and enjoy it. It is played by professional musicians called Ragis. They are skilled performers, who travel around to different gurdwaras. As well as traditional instruments, they play harmoniums, which were taken to India from Britain and are much loved there. Nowadays, however, many young Sikhs prefer Indian film and pop music.

MUSIC IN A GURDWARA

Professional Ragis work in groups of three. One plays a portable harmonium and another plays the drum or drums. They may use Indian *tabla* drums, or a Panjabi drum called a *dholak*. The third musician usually sings the *Gurbani* (poetry) and explains it, and he may also play an instrument. But Sikhs do not need to have professionals there to sing. Anyone can take part if they want to, and some Sikhs play regularly. In most gurdwaras, young people can have lessons and are encouraged to play, like the children in this photograph.

INDIAN MUSIC

Indian music is not written down. Trained musicians make up the music around *ragas*, which are tunes with about five or seven notes. The ragas have different moods: for instance, they can be happy, sad or peaceful. Ragas are also suitable for different times of day or seasons. (There are spring and autumn moods.) Thirty-one different ragas are used in the Guru Granth Sahib.

BHANGRA DANCING

Bhangra dancing is a traditional Panjabi harvest dance. It was done when the crop was safely gathered. The farmers tied bells on their ankles and put on brightly coloured clothes. Some men beat drums and the others circled, stamping their feet and clapping their hands. As the dance went on, it became faster and noisier, ending in a mad whirl, before everyone fell down exhausted.

INSTRUMENTS

Punjabis like *dholaks*, drums that are struck at both ends. Large ones are beaten with drumsticks and small ones are played with the hands. Dancers attach *gungroos* (bells) to their ankles, and people often use clappers and instruments like tambourines.

Dholak

POP MUSIC

Filmi music, the pop music that is an essential part of Indian films, is a favourite with all Indians. Young people also enjoy pop music of any kind. Indian and Western pop music have influenced each other. Bhangra mixed with disco music is called 'Bhangra beat' and has been enormously popular with young Panjabis and others. Some young Sikhs are expert rappers.

·DO·SIKHS· ·LIKE· STORIES?

Panjab is a land where people love stories. They like stories with a moral. For example, there's the one about the crow who was tricked into singing by the crafty fox and dropped her cheese. Then there is the tale of the brothers who were shown how easy it is to break a single stick and how hard it is to break a bundle of sticks, which taught them that they should work together. Sikhs also enjoy stories about the wit and wisdom of famous and holy men. Their favourite stories are love stories. The one they like best is the tale of Hir and Ranjha. Everyone knows what happened, so the listeners' enjoyment is like the fun of seeing a pantomime – they know what is coming next and enjoy the telling.

THE GURU'S PALM PRINT

This picture tells a story about Guru Nanak. The Guru was travelling with his friend Mardana, who was thirsty. Guru Nanak told him to climb a nearby hill, as there was a holy man, a Wali, at the top who had a well. Mardana climbed up, but the Wali refused him water. This happened three times. The Wali asked why the Guru didn't give Mardana water himself, if he was such a powerful person. Mardana was almost dead from thirst, so the Guru struck the ground with his staff. Immediately, water came up out of the ground and there was water everywhere! Now the Wali discovered he had no water and, in fury, threw a great boulder at the Guru. The Guru stopped it with his outstretched palm, and the palm print is on the rock to this day. There is a gurdwara at the place where this happened, at Hassan Abdal in Pakistan.

THE STORY OF HIR AND RANJHA

Ranjha was the youngest of his family. One day, he was sitting playing his flute when his brothers' wives passed by. They said that he was lazy, playing music and not working, They told him that with his airs and graces he should go and find Hir, a woman famous for her beauty, and win her love.

As soon as they told him about Hir, Ranjha felt that he loved her. So he set off to find her. He had a difficult journey, but was blessed by five holy men.

Eventually, he came to the place where Hir lived and saw her. She really was very beautiful.

Ranjha told her his story and played his flute. His music was enchanting, and Hir fell in love with him. She found him a job caring for the village cows and buffaloes. In the afternoons, Hir would meet Ranjha. He would play the flute and talk of love.

This happiness could not last. Hir's uncle, a spiteful man called Kaido, began to spy on the couple and to gossip.

He went and told Hir's parents. The parents were furious and sacked Ranjha. Hir went to Kaido's house, smashed all his pots and set the place alight.

Hir's parents decided to marry Hir to another man, called Saida. The two had been betrothed as children, and so the wedding was arranged very quickly. Hir cried as they took her away.

Ranjha went up into the mountains and became a Yogi, a holy man.

There were celebrations at Saida's house after the marriage, but Saida's sister, Sehti, discovered that her new sister-in-law was not a happy woman. Then a flute-playing Yogi came to the area. He was said to be a great healer. Hir pretended that she had been bitten by a snake, and the holy man was sent for to heal her. Hir knew that the man was Ranjha. As soon as they were alone they were in each other's arms.

Hir and Ranjha made a plan, with the help of Sehti. They ran away together. Saida's family pursued the lovers, but they reached a court where it was decided that Hir's marriage to Saida was no true marriage, since Hir had never agreed to it. Hir and Ranjha were free to marry.

Happy at last, the couple went to Hir's family home, and Hir stayed there whilst Ranjha went to invite his relatives to the wedding.

The preparations for the ceremony began, but Hir's parents knew that everyone had seen Hir leave with Saida's family and that now, if everyone saw her leave with a second man, it would look immoral. They decided to poison Hir. One day they gave her a drink, and moments later she fell to the ground, calling out Ranjha's name with her dying breath.

A message was sent to Ranjha, and he hurried back to find out what was wrong. When he saw Hir's tomb, he realised she was dead. Unable to bear the grief, Ranjha also fell dead upon her grave.

HIDDEN MEANINGS

Although Panjabi folk tales like the story of Hir and Ranjha seem to be just romantic stories, they do have a message. Many people believe the tales are allegories, or symbolic stories, and that the lovers represent God and the soul. The two always get separated and they suffer dreadfully. Sikh Gurus and other religious teachers say that a person has to love God as strongly as the lovers love each other in order to know Him properly. And the love is no easy option: it may mean a lot of pain.

CHILDREN READING

Sikh children, like the ones in this photograph, often enjoy reading traditional Indian stories. There are legends, myths and fables about romantic heroes, kings and warriors, monsters and strong men. There are tales of wit and trickery. They read about the Gurus, and also about the holy men of other religions. In olden times, bards used to go and sing these stories at villages. These days, there are illustrated books, comics and television series.

·GLOSSARY·

AKHAND PATH A continuous reading of the whole of the Guru Granth Sahib.

AMRIT Nectar, the sweetened water drunk at Khalsa initiation ceremonies.

ARDAS The Sikh prayer, said at all Sikh ceremonies.

BHANGRA A traditional harvest dance.

CASTE The Indian class or social division.

CHAUR A sign of royalty, a whisk that is waved above respected persons or the Guru Granth Sahib.

DHOLAK A folk drum played in Panjab.

DIWALI The Indian festival of light, which happens in autumn.

DIWAN The court of a king. A Sikh congregation sits as if it is a royal court.

GRANTHIS People who take care of the gurdwara and the Guru Granth Sahib.

GURBANI The Gurus' poetry.

GURDWARA The place where Sikhs meet for religious and social occasions.

GURPURBS The anniversaries of the births and deaths of the Gurus and of the installing of the first Guru Granth Sahib.

GURU God, as He communicates with humans, or a human Sikh teacher.

GURU GRANTH SAHIB The holy book, which is now the Guru.

HARMANDIR SAHIB, DARBAR SAHIB Names for the Golden Temple at Amritsar.

INITIATION A special ceremony in which someone joins a group or organisation.

JATHEDAR The head of one of the Takhats, a paid official.

KACHH An undergarment, one of the five Ks.

KANGHA A comb, one of the five Ks.

KARA An iron bangle, one of the five Ks.

KARAH PRASAD Special food offered to everyone at gurdwaras.

KAUR A name given to Sikh women.

KES Uncut hair, one of the five Ks.

KHALSA The community started by the tenth Guru.

KHANDA A double-edged sword. Also the name of the Sikh symbol.

KIRPAN A curved sword, one of the five Ks.

KIRTAN Singing of the Guru's poems, as hymns.

LANGAR The Guru's kitchen, where food is served to everyone.

MALA A necklace or rosary.

MANJI The Guru Granth Sahib's throne.

MELA A fair.

MIRI Power in the world. (See Piri.)

NISHAN SAHIB The flag that flies over gurdwaras.

PAHUL The Sikh initiation ceremony.

PAINTI The Panjabi alphabet.

PANGAT Eating in lines in which everyone is equal.

PANJ PIARE The Five Beloved Ones, the first members of the Khalsa.

PIRI Spiritual power. (See Miri.)

RAGA An Indian musical scale.

RUMALA A beautiful cloth which is draped over the Guru Granth Sahib.

SANGAT The Sikh congregation.

SEVA Service to the community, such as cleaning the gurdwara, cooking, guarding shoes.

SINGH The title given to a male Sikh.

TAKHAT One of the 'thrones', centres of government of Sikhism.

VAISAKHI The festival celebrating the anniversary of the founding of the Khalsa.

· I N D E X ·